The Manager's Pocket Guide to Public Presentations

Steve Gladis, Ph.D.

HRD Press ❖ Amherst, MA

Published by:
  HRD Press, Inc.
  22 Amherst Road
  Amherst, Massachusetts 01002
  1-800-822-2801 (U.S. and Canada)
  (413) 253-3488
  (413) 253-3490 (fax)
  http://www.hrdpress.com

Production services by Jean Miller
Cover design by Eileen Klockars

ISBN 0-87425-470-1

*Dedicated
to Dad*

TABLE OF CONTENTS

PREFACE

Public speaking is as important today as it's ever been and perhaps even more so. When you think about how much impact television has had by transmitting a speech presented before a few hundred people to an audience of millions, it is staggering to consider that a local speech might become national news in a matter of moments.

But, speaking has always been important for several reasons. First, because it can reach a large group of people simultaneously. Second, because it often inspires people to do something. And third, because the speaker has so much at stake, personally, in the speech. In fact, in a recent survey, people were asked to list their greatest fears in life and to rank them. Public speaking was ranked number one—even ahead of death!

The Manager's Pocket Guide to Public Presentations is *not* a lot of things. It is not a textbook. It is not the first or final word on public speaking. It is not the cure for pre-speaking jitters. It *is* a compendium of tips that will help any manager learn the survival tactics of public speaking. It is a simple, quick read, based on the accepted theory and practice of rhetoric. It is a confidence builder and will help you to begin to overcome speaking anxiety. Here is a brief look at the ten chapters:

The first rule, *"Think Before You Speak,"* explores your basic option as a speaker: To speak or not. As simple as this sounds, it involves some big considerations: your company's objectives; your comfort, time and ability; and the group itself. The decision to speak is an important one, and should be made intelligently.

The second rule, *"Analyze Your Speech Commitment,"* looks at what you must do immediately after accepting a speech. Comprehensive analysis of the group, of the occasion, of your objectives, and of audience expectations is vital early on to provide direction and meaning to your speech.

The third rule, *"Research Your Speech,"* dives into the speech itself and covers choosing a topic of interest to you and the audience, developing a thesis, interviewing people in the collection and research phase to save you time and effort, and discovering what files and resources will help you, as a public speaker—all of which may be at your fingertips.

The fourth rule, *"Create an Outline,"* discusses a fundamental construction for any speaker: the outline. This chapter covers the rationale for an outline. It also provides the basic, tried and true three-part structure for any speech. And, it will offer a variety of structural tips to help you design an outline that will make sense to you and ultimately to your audience.

The fifth rule, *"Pretest Your Outline,"* provides the public speaker with a safety net. It introduces the concept of a peer group with whom to test your speech before you give it in public. This chapter will show you how differing points of view help strengthen your speech. It will also discuss how to structure a meeting with peers and how to edit speeches without losing friends. Self editing, one-on-one editing and the use of subject-matter experts round out this most important chapter.

The sixth rule, *"Write Out the Speech Draft,"* provides several tactics for quickly getting your ideas on paper. In particular, it introduces both a writing and a speaking technique that can help produce a written draft in short order. This chapter also offers speech-writing tips and techniques to help make the speech work for you, the speaker, and flow for the audience.

The seventh rule, *"Make Your Presentation,"* discusses what to do before you speak to help you physically and mentally prepare for the speech. It also focuses on several nonverbal techniques to enhance any speech.

The eighth rule, *"Be Prepared for Anything,"* stresses a number of key preparation steps and provides tips to handle the two types of unforeseen but inevitable speeches: impromptu and introductory speeches.

The ninth rule, *"Answer Questions from the Audience,"* deals with taking questions from the audience. Questions are inescapable for any speaker, but how you answer them may be crucial to how you are accepted as a speaker. This chapter will help you navigate through the potentially explosive minefield of Q and A sessions.

The tenth rule, *"Publicize Your Speech,"* recognizes that: it ain't over till it's over, and even when it's over, it's still not over! This

chapter discusses what to do before and after your speech to ensure that your speech has a life after presentation.

THE FIRST RULE:

*Think Before
You Speak*

To quote Woody Allen, "Having money is better than poverty, if only for financial reasons." Indeed, the bottom line in business is money. Whether you're talking about spending money for new furniture, new cars or new widgets—it all boils down to cost effectiveness. So too, with public presentations. You can and *must* put a price tag on public speaking because it will cost you, as a manager and the public speaker, and your company, as the sponsor, money to present your speech to an audience.

However, rarely do businesses give the same attention to decision making for speeches that is given to purchasing a piece of equipment of far less expense. Why? Possibly because there are so many hidden "time costs." There's research time, speechwriter time (if you're so lucky), personal time—at home thinking about the speech—travel expenses, time away from the job, downtime at airports, in taxis, on trains, planes and boats! The list goes on and on. When you tally it all up—which is rarely done—it's a chunk of time and money. And time is the one thing that managers have the least of; thus, it is the most valued—time truly is money.

If the bottom line is important, then we ought to develop a method for decision making and ask some key questions regarding speeches. This chapter will explore the critical questions a manager should answer before accepting a speaking engagement.

WHO IS THE AUDIENCE?

Perhaps the most basic, and yet the most overlooked critical question concerns the audience. For example, if it's Congress or the stockholders, is there any doubt that you should speak? Hardly. The audience determines the decision in such obvious cases. But what about the more common and less obvious groups?

When you receive an invitation to speak, your principal objective should be to qualify the group. You must determine who they are so you can decide if it will be worth your, and the company's, time to speak to them. So how do you qualify the group?

First, check company files and see if you have any in-house information or analysis about the group already on hand. Often overlooked, in-house files can provide a rich information resource to help you decide. Second, talk with other speakers (and your speakers bureau if you have one) to determine if anyone in the company has ever addressed the group before. There are nothing like firsthand experiences, especially when it comes to speeches. Third, check out any number of references like the Internet, *Standard and Poors, The Reader's Guide to Periodical Literature, The Business Index, Nexus,* etc. Finally, if it's a group or association, be sure to check *The Encyclopedia of Associations* for an excellent synopsis of organizations and associations around the country.

If you're still in doubt after such preliminary research, then take the direct approach and call the person who invited you. Better yet, meet her or him face to face. Such personal encounters can give you great insight into the group and make decision making much easier. Ask about the group: its make-up, background, likes and dislikes. Discuss former speakers whom the group enjoyed and why. Find out how long you would be expected to speak and certainly if there will be any other speakers before or after your speech. Get a copy of the proposed agenda to see where you would come in the program.

WHAT IS THE PURPOSE OF THE SPEECH?

One of the preliminary questions you should always ask the group's representative is what is the purpose of the speech: to inform, persuade or entertain.

Speeches to Inform

Speeches to inform represent the bulk of public speeches and, therefore, should be considered a top priority in this process. When considering a speech to inform, you need to think about facts, information and data. Simply put, you must consider what you and the audience know about the subject and how to make your information interesting. Effective informational speeches provide relevant information to audiences. For some speakers this may mean talking on a subject of which they have little initial knowledge. This can translate into mounds of reading and assimilation, briefings and report reviews—often just to get to the level of the average person in the audience.

Advice: Don't give a speech to inform on a topic on which you have little information unless a subject-matter expert has helped to prepare the speech.

Speeches to Persuade

Speeches to persuade rely on reasoning, more so than facts. Surely facts support the reasons, but the primary objective is to persuade—to get people to think differently or to do something that you want. To persuade thinking people you must present a firm position that is buttressed by logical reasons, which are in turn supported by accurate information. Persuasion is a higher order of thinking than information because it draws conclusions. Therefore, it takes more preparation and analysis. What does this mean to a public speaker? More work. If you want to persuade effectively, you'll have to know clearly where you stand on an issue and accurately support it. In addition, you must also know your audience's stance on the issue so that you can work from their position toward your position.

Advice: Choose these speeches carefully; they can be dangerous in the world of public speaking.

Speeches to Entertain

Speeches to entertain are perhaps the most difficult of all the three types of general speeches because while humor is universal— taste in humor is very much individual. Thus, it's easy to bomb when trying to deliver what is for you a very funny speech, or even to deliver only a funny story within a speech. Again, knowing the audience's culture and background, which will be discussed later in this book, will help the speaker hit the mark more directly. A good place to employ a speech to entertain is with a safe audience whose culture and background you understand: an internal audience. Certainly, it is appropriate at a retirement or corporate party to inject humor, but in this case you, as a speaker, have the inside story and know the culture. So give it a try. But with an unknown audience, use caution.

Advice: Be very careful with speeches to entertain unless you know the culture well and background of the audience very well. When in doubt leave such speeches to comedians.

WHAT'S IN IT FOR ME?

Because a speech places the speaker at risk, if only in front of the audience, then it stands to reason the speaker should get some personal payback. At the very least, the speaker's personal objectives should be con- sidered when choosing a speech. Some might say that a paycheck should suffice, but because speeches take considerably more than 9-to-5 preparation and worry, more speaker consideration seems appropriate. So what should be considered? First, influence. The speaker might consider personal visibility created by the speech. A pivotal speech in the industry may set the speaker up as an expert in the field, thus making herself and the business respected and valued in a particular community or sphere of influence.

Second, location. Remember the old real estate adage about the three most important points about buying property: "Location, location, location." Well, location of a speech might also be another consideration for the speaker— even a perk. For example, a speech in Phoenix in January as opposed to August might rate as high as a speech in Maine in August versus the same speech in January. Further, as a speaker you may want to look over a location as a possible future job site. You may want to visit family, friends or take the family on a much-needed vacation—all of which answer the question: What's in it for me?

WHAT'S IN IT FOR MY COMPANY?

As a public speaker for your company, you must always consider the speech's importance to the company you represent—the organization which pays your salary. Indeed, what are some of the reasons why companies should pay to send speakers to address specific audiences?

❖ **To establish a personal bond between the company and the audience.**

For many reasons, companies need to establish personal links with an audience. Perhaps there has been a rift in the past. Maybe there has never been a strong tie and now, because of the times, one is necessary. Whatever the reason, companies can solidify linkages with audiences by providing a living, breathing person to speak rather than a sterile report or memorandum. By personalizing the bond through a public speaker, years of hostility or misunderstanding can be overcome— not a bad cost tradeoff for any organization.

❖ **To open channels of communication.**

As a direct follow-up on the first reason, facilitating communication prompted by sending a personal emissary cannot be overlooked. Often as a result of a speech, the company obtains a person to call and ask questions—a personal contact. Dialogue between your organization and the audience can begin, and it can cut through confusion and misunderstanding in the future.

❖ **To set company policy.**

Speeches have always been a rich source to provide forums to espouse company policy. Because they are recorded and often written, or at least transcribed, speeches offer organizations a permanent record of company policy which can guide other managers and personnel as they attempt to accurately represent the company in public. Additionally, such speeches can help set the tone, direction and values of the corporation. Delivered in public settings— often amplified with media presence—speeches can set the agenda for organizational policy and culture.

❖ **To attract media attention.**

Speeches have long been a way to release new information and themes to the media.

Politicians, for example, have used the medium of speech giving to set in motion new themes like "The Great Society," "The New Frontier" and "The Thousand Points of Light." Rhetoric has been a tradition in our society, and it will always attract coverage. Thus, companies can also use such occasions to capitalize on the events to advertise their position, product or people.

So, What's the Bottom Line?

Well, it's often not an easy call. All of the above factors must be considered when choosing a speech. However, it all boils down to: Is it worth it? Are the hours of preparation, the costs, the time away from operations worth the objectives—both personal and corporate? In fact, is this audience worth the effort? These sound like cold and callous questions, but they are merely practical. The cost of doing business, whether private or public, escalates every year. So, all must be mindful of such costs when deciding what to do.

One way to help make this decision is to reverse the trend of waiting for speech invitations to come to you, and to target the audiences from whom you think both you and your organization would most likely benefit. A simple, but effective strategy, this approach is used by few organizations. Why? One can only speculate. Many organizations don't want to appear to be soliciting for speeches—it may seem beneath their dignity.

The reality is that many groups would not consider public speakers from certain corporations because they simply wouldn't think of them. For example, the National Education Association (NEA) may not think of an individual from the consumer products division of Ford or from the U.S. Treasury to speak, when in fact both organizations may well have a connection or topic of vital interest to the NEA. By reaching out, corporations can better obtain their objectives and avoid the sit-back-and-wait syndrome. Moreover, by targeting major speeches to be given in the upcoming year, organizations can set their own travel priorities rather than let smaller, less important speech requests set their agenda. This type of direct, aggressive speech program ensures "more bang for the buck." After all, we must always consider the *bottom line.*

THE SECOND RULE:

*Analyze Your
Speech
Commitment*

Once your have made the decision to speak to a particular group, the work begins. Like the journey of a thousand miles, it must begin with the first step: analysis. Few important ventures are worth it without prior analysis. As the saying goes, "When you're up to your elbows in alligators, it's very hard to remember that the reason you waded into the swamp was to drain it!"

Before you wade in, analyze the situation to help you spot any alligators that might look like innocent logs floating around. This chapter will look at the types of analysis you might want to conduct prior to drafting your speech. Specifically, it will cover analyzing the audience, the occasion and your principal objective.

ANALYZE THE AUDIENCE

An audience is like a large corporate body—in fact, you will do well to consider a speech as a conversation with a large, conglomerate person, comprised of all the personalities within the group. And like any "person," an audience with common interests shares common or similar attitudes, values, beliefs and opinions. The audience also has a selfish need to be fed the kind of information in which it has an interest. In essence, the effective speaker must address the audience on its own terms, always keeping in mind, "What you can do for the audience." Let's analyze some of the characteristics of any audience you might encounter.

First, *consider the audience's interest in your topic.* In teaching, this is called the "teachable moment." Frankly, if students or audiences are not at a teachable or receptive moment, the best you can hope for on their part is the civility that they won't throw tomatoes—at least not too hard. Seriously, you must determine the level of interest in the topic. You can do so by interviewing your host—the person who invited you or whoever your audience contact is. Communicate frequently with such a contact person, so that you get a feel for who the audience is well before speech day.

Let's consider the worst case scenario: The audience is not that interested in your topic. Let's also assume that you still have to speak to them and cannot get out of the situation—which would be the best choice in such a situation. Then make the speech short.

Audiences appreciate brevity, especially when they are bored. Remember this speech adage: If you are brief, you'll be considered good; if you are brief and good, you'll be considered great.

Second, in keeping with interest in the topic, *consider how much the audience knows about the topic*. Obviously, you'll speak differently to a group of experts than to novices on a given topic. Be especially careful of jargon you may be tempted to use, because often, what is common language to those who are experts in the field, are empty words to newcomers. If you are in doubt about how much the audience knows, treat it as an "intelligent ignorant"—someone who is intelligent but merely ignorant of your area of expertise. Treat them with respect and do not talk down to them. At the same time, recognize that you cannot assume they know as much as you do.

Third, *consider the audience's attitude toward the topic.* Although this could be considered along with interest, because it is so important, it should be considered on its own. Most important for the speaker is to learn whether or not the audience actually has hostility for the topic. Certainly, speaking to a hostile audience requires skills and strategies that go beyond the average speech. If you do discover hostility, try to find out reasons why it exists and just as important, try to determine as specifically as possible what exactly the audience's position is on your topic. For example, if you're speaking about pro-union options for workers and the audience is absolutely opposed to unions under any circumstances, then your job as a speaker is much more difficult. The starting position for a speaker who wants to reach an audience is largely determined by where the audience's position is, not just the speaker's.

Fourth, *consider audience characteristics:* age, education, background, gender, socio-economic status, etc. No need to belabor the obvious, but any speaker, whether in simple conversation or delivering a speech, must consider the factors listed above to relate to the audience on its terms. You filter what you say in normal conversation through these considerations quite naturally, without ever thinking. For example, when explaining some-thing to a child, most people will, without thinking, automatically adjust their vocabulary to the educational level of the child. However, oftentimes those same people, when delivering a speech, forget the fundamental adjustments we naturally make in conversation. To avoid this mistake, consider your speech a conversation with a composite body called an audience, and your presentation will go well. In short, consider the basics of good, relevant conversation.

ANALYZE THE OCCASION

Often overlooked, the occasion of the speech itself provides the speaker with direction and insight into the speech. Quite simply one might ask, "Why am I being asked to speak?" It could be an annual retraining session, an after dinner speech at a social meeting, a retirement luncheon, a stockholders meeting, induction of new club members or a thousand other reasons. Whatever those reasons, the speaker needs to be aware of the timing, the location and the immediate events surrounding the speech.

For example, timing is everything in life — or so we're told. So it is with speeches. When asked to deliver a speech, you should always be aware of the context in which the speech will take place. *What are the events of the day?* For example, you may be giving a speech on oil and petroleum products, but fail to read the morning's paper which shows a $2-a-barrel increase in crude. Try to guess what will be the first question you might get after you finish your speech. Guess also how you'll feel when your answer is, "I was unaware the price had gone up today."

Another relevant factor to your speech could be *what has your organization done recently that could have an impact on your speech.* Let's say, for example, that a week prior to your speech before the American Ethics Society, your company treasurer is indicted for fraud. You should know the details of that matter to help you handle the obvious questions that will come.

What events in your own life might relate to your speech? Perhaps you have just had a child and happen to be talking to the International Association of Child Care Givers. The recent birth of your child and your obvious concern for the industry helps develop credibility among your audience immediately.

Equally as important is location. Consider that you've been invited to speak at an annual fund-raiser for a homeless shelter in the inner city of a large metropolitan area. Doing your homework always helps. Knowing something about the current developments and historical background of the inner city will duly impress your audience. A quick trip to the public library to educate yourself about the area's history will provide you with facts that will ensure that you are perceived as a knowledgeable and concerned corporate speaker.

Also, one of the best ways to familiarize yourself with a location is to visit the site before you speak. This sounds simple, but visiting the location of the speech in advance is often the most overlooked strategy in delivering a speech. Certainly, this takes a fair amount of effort on your part and for certain out-of-town speeches it is difficult if not impossible. However, if at all feasible, such a visit can help to psychologically prepare you for your speech and can help provide a concrete image for you to work with when you rehearse your speech. In addition, knowing how to get to the location, the surrounding, the size of the room, the lighting, and the acoustics gives you added confidence and audience awareness necessary in delivering an effective speech. However, even if you cannot visit the site in advance, you can still visit it prior to your speech.

Arriving an hour or so before your speech is also absolutely essential. If you don't, the consequences can be grave. First, you may encounter traffic delays or simply have difficulty finding the place. Second, you may discover that because the air conditioning is not working, it's 95 degrees in the room. Therefore, an early arrival may also allow you time to get the room cooled down or provide you time to cut your speech to 3 minutes— about the amount of time anyone could stay awake under those conditions! An early arrival will also give you time to get an updated situation report from your host about the audience, such as their present attitude, what has immediately preceded your remarks, any late-breaking problems, concerns and so on. Always remember, it's better to be there 1 hour early than 10 minutes late.

ANALYZE YOUR PRINCIPAL OBJECTIVE

Every speech should have a single, over-riding objective. While you may have your personal agenda and the company its objectives, as a public speaker you must decide on a principal objective: What do you want the audience to think or do differently as a result of your speech? Having such a single objective sounds simple enough, but few, if any, speakers ever write down or formally articulate that principal objective.

To accomplish this task, simply take out an index card and finish the following sentence: "When I step down from the podium, I would like the members of the audience to..." Your answer might be: "To write to their congressional representatives." "To endorse our new company policy." "To more clearly understand our organizational commitment to the consumer." Notice that the more concrete your action, the more you will be able to gauge your effectiveness as a speaker. For example, it will be easier to know how many people write their congressmen (if they send you a copy of the letter) than it will be to know how well they understand your organization's commitment to the consumer—unless, of course, you give them a pop quiz! Thus, the more concrete and visual an objective, the more easily evaluated. Regardless of how concrete the objective, at least have one, preferably written down, so you can refer to it, modify it or toss it out for a better one as you begin wading into preparing the text of your speech.

THE THIRD RULE:

Research Your
Speech

Research is like digging for gold: You have to turn over tons of dirt to uncover those few, precious nuggets that make it all worthwhile. But, you must believe that if a speech is worth giving, then uncovering tons of dirt for the few great speech nuggets is just part of your commitment, as a speaker, to your audience. Many speakers would willingly make the effort, but simply do not know how. This chapter will focus on research, from selecting your topic, to conducting preliminary research, developing a thesis, and re-researching your subject. Each step in this process brings you closer to a final polished speech.

CHOOSING THE TOPIC

Imagine going on vacation. The car is packed and you're ready to roll, but one thing has been forgotten: the destination. That may sound ludicrous—after all, how would you have packed accordingly or known how much money to take out of the bank?

Researching a public speech should be at least as rigorous as going on vacation (although probably not as much fun)—you should always have a destination in mind when you start. However, for most speakers, coming up with the original idea, the destination, is difficult. So let's discuss how to choose a destination that won't get you lost along the way.

One strategy for choosing a speech topic is simply to speak on a topic in which you're very interested. If you are going to spend hours putting a speech together, it might as well be on a topic you truly enjoy. Of course, you should always try to merge your area of interest with the audience's. You do this by contacting the host or some representative of the group who is coordinating the speech.

Invariably, if the speech did not result from your own telephone call, there will be a person's name and phone number associated with each speech. Contact that individual and discuss topics in which the audience would have high interest. You'll be surprised how much you will learn from a single phone call. Better yet, where possible, meet with your host in person to assess more accurately his or her honest reactions to your topic proposals. For example, suppose you were going to speak on the impact of industry on the environment, and just last week the Secretary of the Interior had given a speech to the same group. Obviously, you can only benefit by testing your topic early with a group representative before you invest hours of time only to find the audience either knows the topic well or is indifferent to it.

Indeed, if you're stuck and can't come up with a topic, such a contact becomes even more important. The audience representative can tell you what topics have gone over well in the past and which have bombed. When you can, avoid topics even remotely related to those that bombed.

A second topic selection strategy is to choose a topic in which you have considerable interest, but would like to explore further. "Speaking to Learn" is an important concept that all public speakers understand. When you prepare to put your ideas on the line—in a public forum—there is a gut-level fear which motivates you to know what you're talking about. That motivation often causes great learning to take place. In fact, many teachers—the ultimate public speakers—will confess that they never really knew a subject until they taught it. There is something compelling, perhaps its a genuine fear of failure, about getting up in front of a group that makes us want to know our subject matter. Thus, you can use the speech to teach yourself.

A third strategy is to develop several canned speeches. Of course, these speeches should be on topics of interest to you and any general audience. By developing such boiler-plate speeches, you stand ready at a moment's notice to give a speech. In fact, many organizations have such speeches on file for managers. Such speeches cut down the research time, assure greater speaker confidence and develop a consistency of information disseminated to the public.

Whatever topic selection strategy you use, remember to choose something in which both you and the audience share a common interest. To find out what the audience likes, you need a sounding board: an audience representative. By using that person as a sounding board for your ideas, you will save time and ensure that your speech will be a success.

CONDUCTING RESEARCH

With a general topic in hand, you'll need to wade into the oceans of information available in today's information-filled society. If any thing, you'll probably be overwhelmed with the amount of information you'll be faced with, especially with the advent of the Internet and computerized databases. So, it might be useful to develop a wading-in method. This section will suggest the following progression: (1) discover what you know; (2) what experts know; and (3) what information systems can provide.

First, discovering what you know is the most overlooked resource in public speaking. People seem to discount the information they know — they think that somehow book information is more valid than personal experience. Not so. In fact, if you're an expert in your field, in all likelihood your information will be much more up to date than a book written 5 or 10 years ago. So why not begin with yourself? Yes, you say, but how? Two ways: freewriting and freelisting.

Freewriting is like writing a letter to a trusted friend about your speech topic. Just as when you write to a friend, you don't worry about the spelling or grammatical errors. You just write to get the information down on paper. So, write a letter to your best friend about your speech. Don't stop to correct spelling or typing errors. Simply tell them what you know about the topic, and do it quickly.

But, maybe this technique, freewriting, isn't one with which you're comfortable. Don't worry; try freelisting. Freelisting is like making a shopping list. Just sit down and make a list. Again, don't worry about how neat or tidy it is. This is a working list and is never going to see the light of an outside audience; so, list away! The idea is to make a list as quickly and as uninterruptedly as you can. Keep the flow of ideas coming and don't stop to correct a word or look up a grammar rule—not at this point in the process. There will be plenty of opportunity for editing later.

Next, discovering what subject-matter experts know is vital to research because it can save you time and cover the territory effectively and efficiently. Imagine how simple research can be if you begin with someone who knows the topic. That's exactly what you do when you begin with experts. Let's say, for example, that you're going to speak on a company program—the sales incentive program. You are familiar with the program but not an expert. Then why not talk with the sales manager and with a few salespeople. Surely the company may have a few policy manuals written on the topic, and they too might be helpful, but before you wade through "what ought to be" you should find out "what is." Subject-matter experts give you that perspective and do it quickly.

They also act as "finders and pointers." They will often find information in their files and give it to you, which saves you vast amounts of research time. They also will point you in the direction of new research they might have read but haven't yet added to their files. For example, they may have seen a new presentation or read a recent journal article which may provide pivotal information to your research. Listening closely to these experts up front will save you hours of work down the line.

Finally, don't overlook the obvious: information systems. First, consider the tremendous power of the Internet and the World Wide Web. By using a basic search engine like Yahoo, Lycos or one of a number of these search engines, you can lay your hands on up-to-date information in seconds. Perhaps the greatest resource people in this area are research librarians. Educated in a discipline focused on finding information, they can also save you hours of groping in the dark by shining well focused lights into the corners of the library. Obviously, there are a wide variety of libraries and librarians. Contact librarians in large public libraries and at university libraries, because they have the most experience, especially in technical topics. Generally, such libraries are well stocked with periodicals and access systems geared toward research because their primary clients, students and professors, continually conduct research.

Neighborhood libraries have neither the orientation nor the staffing to sustain high levels of research professionals. Even so, good research can still be done locally. It only means that if you have access to a city or university library, don't pass it by. By the way, most college or university libraries are open to the public, but do not allow borrowing books unless you are enrolled, an alumnus or on staff. However, their complete range of services is readily available from electronic databases to microfiche documents.

Don't overlook corporate librarians or association libraries either. First, most major corporations have their own library and hire someone to maintain it. Whether certified librarians or not, be sure to get to know them and put them on the alert that you will be writing a speech on a particular topic. Second, this country has over 4,000 associations. To find out what association you might want to consult, use *The Encyclopedia of Associations* (available in most libraries). The *Encyclopedia* has entries by subject topic and name. It provides valuable information on the size, organization and areas of expertise of the association and is a most comprehensive guide in this area. Associations also maintain libraries—some more extensive than others. Association librarians can be helpful about giving you the latest information in the field. After all, as an industry representative, the availability of all current information on a selected topic is one of their critical functions.

Within each library, no matter how large or small, there exist systems of information. It may be as simple as a card catalog and copies of the *Reader's Guide to Periodical Literature* or as sophisticated as online resources and computerized databases. Getting to know how to use these systems is crucial to good research. For example, in many sophisticated university libraries a variety of databases can be accessed thoroughly and quickly. To illustrate, you may be writing a speech on the topic of developing effective training programs in business and industry. By getting access to a business periodicals database, you will be able to pull out numerous references and a 100 to 150 word abstract of each article in a matter of seconds. All of this saves time and helps focus your efforts on the topic.

DEVELOPING A THESIS

One advantage of early and quick access to information systems is to help you further define and refine your speech's central focal point: the thesis. Your thesis is the "bottom line" of your speech. When you strip away all the words and the superstructure, the thesis is the essence. Generally, you should be able to express a thesis in one simple, well-thought-out declarative sentence, and it should flow from the topic in a directional manner. For example, let's say you were speaking on the topic of public relations, but you wanted to address a particular aspect such as how to handle a hostile television interview. Your thesis for an informative speech might be: To be successful in a hostile television interview, you need to know certain strategies. Thus, what would naturally follow would be a discussion about the individual strategies—what they are and how they work.

RESEARCHING WITH A THESIS

Research is a re-cursive and dynamic process. It can be one of discovery, as well. Just when you think you know it all, you uncover a new piece of information or research that makes the puzzle clearer. Certainly, after you've refined your topic down to your thesis, it's time to rethink and reprocess information you have already collected and think about going back to original sources. With your more refined thesis in hand, use it like a flashlight in the dark to help you discover facts and ideas. With a thesis, research tends to be more directed, specific and clear.

To illustrate, let's consider that you conducted preliminary research on the topic of recycled paper. During your research you collected all kinds of facts and ideas on the topic. After sifting through them and talking with your audience representative, you formulated a tentative thesis as follows: Companies can save money while conserving natural resources by using recycled paper. Now armed with this thesis to light the way, you delve back into your resources and suddenly facts and ideas relevant to your thesis jump off the page because your focal point has become more direct—your light is focused and stronger. Thus, a particular cost-effectiveness study conducted by a Canadian consulting firm on the economics of recycled paper may have much more relevance now than it did in your preliminary research.

Don't be afraid to revise your research according to the thesis you've developed. Time has not been wasted. It's all part of the learning process, and the very way you become familiar with and master information. Not only will your thesis help your continuing research, it will have a great impact on organizing your speech, which will be discussed in the next chapter.

THE FOURTH RULE:

Create an Outline

A speech should never be a treasure hunt for your audience. They should not have to work hard to understand your ideas. You can help them and yourself by organizing a structure that ensures that they won't get lost. The heart of that structure begins with the outline—a speechwriter's best friend. The outline strips away the camouflage of words and leaves only the essence of the concepts, so that you can inspect how they all fit together— their logic and sequence within the speech.

This chapter will focus on the outline in detail. Specifically, it will discuss: First, who should use an outline and why; and second, the process of putting an outline together. Further, throughout the chapter the discussion will raise the notion and importance of organization and structure within speeches.

THE WHO AND WHY OF AN OUTLINE

Question: Who should use an outline?

Answer: Anyone who wants to make sure that the speech is organized logically and that it is both complete and proportioned. Are there people who write speeches without using an outline? Yes. But it's a pay-me-now-or-pay-me-later proposition. You can either create order up front and then move forward or create order later. But, you must provide order at some point if you want the audience to understand and enjoy your speech.

Whether you are an experienced, professional public speaker or a rank amateur, the outline will keep your ideas organized and logical. No audience gives any speaker a grant of immunity with respect to logic, organization or comprehension. Of course, if you're famous you may get a couple of extra minutes of grace period before they turn to reading their newspapers, doodling or walking out on you. But, as a rule, order is expected—even demanded—by the audience, no matter who you are.

Remember those roadside restaurant placemats that have a large haystack drawn on them and underneath it says: "There are 15 faces of Presidents of the United States hidden within this haystack. See if you can find all 15." Everyone knows the purpose of such an exercise: To stall for time and to keep the kids busy until the overworked or undermotivated server can take your order. But when you're writing a speech and you take the haystack-

with-the-hidden-faces approach, you are almost
guaranteed dissatisfied customers.

Question: Why an outline?
Answer: Two reasons. First, because an
audience expects order. Just think about it.
When you hear a speaker, whether in church or
at a political rally, whether a lecturer at a university or someone on television—do you
expect that they will be confusing and disor-
ganized? Absolutely not. You have to believe
that they have credibility as speakers which
boils down to being honest and prepared.
Preparation means having their facts straight
and having those facts in an organizational
pattern that makes sense.

Second, you use an outline because it can
make your speechwriting much easier. Try
building a house without a foundation or worse
yet, without any blueprint or plan. The result:
disaster, disorganization, and finally, despair.
Building a speech without an outline is no less
frustrating. With an outline you can see where
you are going without the unnecessary
baggage of all the text which tends to hide the
cracks in the foundation. When your speech is
stripped bare to the outline you'll quickly see if
an important part is left out, if things are out of

logical order, or if the whole piece is out of proportion. Outlines save time by diagnosing problems early in the speechwriting process, thus avoiding major rewrites later when it's more difficult and more time consuming. Again, it's the old pay-me-now-or-pay-me-later idea. By paying the price early, with the effort of producing an outline, the payment later is minimal, if at all.

THE HOW OF AN OUTLINE

Just how do you go about producing an outline? This section will look at both external and internal organization to make sense of outline construction.

External Order

All outlines follow a basic external structure: introduction, body and conclusion. Let's take them in order and break them down.

The Introduction

Its purpose is to draw audience attention to the topic, to create a need to know for the audience and to structure the forthcoming speech. In a nutshell, the purpose of the introduction is to tell the audience what you're about to tell them! Structurally that consists of four parts: The attention getter, the need to know, the thesis and the preview.

Getting Attention

Attention getters come in many different sizes and shapes. They appear at the very beginning of a speech and come in the form of short stories, hypothetical situations, startling statistics, humor, a demonstration or any device that causes the audience to focus its attention on the speech and not on lunch, dinner or cocktails. For example, a speech about conserving rain forests might start with this hypothetical situation: "Let's pretend for a moment that every tree in the world were cut down and used for building houses or making pulp paper. Do you have any idea how long it would be before we all died of carbon dioxide overdoses or ozone complications? Not long, I can assure you. Did you know that trees filter the air we breath and...."

Another possible opening might involve the use of a demonstration technique: using a single candle burning in a dimly lit room. You begin to talk about the need for clean power sources versus the need for light in our lives as the house lights gradually come up. Indeed, your imagination is the only thing that can limit your introductions. Also, don't forget that you can combine these by using a story along with startling statistics or any useful combination you can imagine. Remember, within your initial outline itself you will only have a brief reference like: "hypothetical story about rain forests." You might also include under this heading a few key words—but keep it brief on an outline.

Establishing the Need to Know

Next, now that you have the audience's attention focused on the topic, you must establish the audience's need to know. Here is where audience analysis will help you greatly. You have to know the relationship of the audience to the topic at hand. How does it affect their lives, what do they think about the topic and so on. For example, you might say to a parent-teacher organization, "Conservation of our rain forests in the Amazon sounds like it's a million miles away until you consider that our children and grandchildren may die if you and I don't do something about it today." There is nothing like focusing an audience's attention on the most important thing in the world to them: themselves and their children.

Developing the Thesis

Then, you need to present the basic thesis of the speech. This can be done by directly telling the audience, "My central point today is that if we continue to allow the wanton harvesting of rain forests for lumber and paper products, we place ourselves and our children at great peril in the *near* future." Remember that the thesis is the bottom line of the speech. It gives force and direction to the speech and, thus, plays a pivotal role in the outline. Don't be misled by its brevity—usually one sentence—because summarizing a speech in one sentence is harder than you would imagine.

Stating the Preview

Now you are ready to preview the entire speech for the audience. In essence you will, "Tell them what you're going to tell them." The preview is simply a road map of the main ideas to come and is introduced in a most direct manner: "This afternoon I'd like to discuss the problem at hand. First, I'll discuss the scope of harvesting that is going on today. Second, I'll try to show how in less than 25 years we will all be in great peril if certain environmental constraints are not practiced. And, finally, I'll offer a few actions you can take to make a difference for your children and this planet." Notice how the preview tells the audience what to expect. It's short, direct but powerful because it gives focus and provides certain expectations to the audience.

If you take the four aspects of the introduction together, they "transform" the audience from a group simply having lunch together to one focused squarely on your topic in four ways: (1) by getting attention: "Let's pretend that every tree in the world was cut down"; (2) by creating a need to know: "Conservation of our rain forests might sound like it's a million miles away until you consider our children"; (3) by stating a thesis: "My central point today is..."; and (4) by previewing the speech: "This afternoon I'd like to discuss the problem at hand. First, I'll discuss..." Your outline of this section of the speech might look like this:

I. Introduction
   A. Hypothetical Situation:
      – Every tree cut down
   B. Need to Know:
      – Threat to us and our children

   C. Thesis:

      Central point is that if we continue the wanton cutting down of trees our lives and those of our children will be in peril.

   D. Preview:
1. Scope of problem
2. The perils ahead
3. Actions to take

The Body

The second part of external organization is the body of the speech. If you can imagine that the thesis is like a bridge, then the body serves as the main support composed of several main ideas or partitions that directly uphold the bridge: the thesis. The main ideas are also introduced, in order, as they were in the preview of the introduction. Thus, in the speech about the rain forests you would have three partitions or main ideas: (1) the current scope of the problem; (2) the perils in the next 25 years; and (3) what actions to take to prevent disaster.

Each of these three main ideas would represent major headings in your outline under which you would develop arguments to support your claims. For example, under the major heading of "The current scope of the problem" you might list certain EPA statistics about the decreasing ozone layer and how decreasing trees causes that layer to get thinner and thinner. You might provide the annual harvest figures for rain forests and graphically show the increasing percentages. You might also note the latest studies from the National Science Coalition showing how the earth's temperature is rising because of the reduced ozone layer and how droughts and famine are directly caused by such a problem. In short, each main idea is a claim which must be supported by as much direct evidence as you can muster.

When you have completed stating and documenting each main idea, you need to make sure that they each directly support the main thesis. Using an outline makes this easy because you have only the briefest of notes under each caption. For example, your outline for the section on the scope of the problem might look like this:

II. The Scope of the Problem
   A. EPA Stats
      1. 1995 study: Ozone layer
         thickness . . .
      2. 1997 study: Ozone layer
         reduced to . . .
   B. 1996-97 Deforestation Study
      1. 7% decrease in trees per year
      2. Economic impact of problem
   C. National Science Coalition Report
      on Rain Forests
      1. Increasing temperatures
      2. Hazards caused: droughts,
         famine . . .

The Conclusion

The third aspect of external organization is the conclusion. Once you've completed the body of your outline and have told the audience what you had promised them in the introduction, then it's time to "Tell them what you told them," by providing the conclusion. The conclusion should include: a cue that you're concluding, a summary of your main points, and a memorable closer—much like the attention getter.

To cue the audience that you are closing, you could say: "In conclusion," or "To summarize what I've talked about today," or any such phrase that will perk them up. To summarize your main points, just hit the high spots; don't redeliver the speech. Finally, regarding the closing, use any of the hints for attention getters or hitchhike on the attention getter you started with for nice closure. Take, for example, the lighted candle you started with. You could end your speech by having someone slowly dimming the lights so that all that is left shining is the solitary candle that you could blow out after saying to the audience: "The choice is ours. We must do something now or the candle in our galaxy that we call earth will be blown out forever." Your outline for the conclusion might look like this:

III. Conclusion
    A. Summarize:
        1. The Problem—destruction of rain forests
        2. Peril in next 25 years
        3. Actions to prevent disaster

    B. Closing:
        1. Choice is ours
        2. Do something, or
        3. Suffer consequences (blow out
            candle)

Internal Structure

With the external structure for your outline in place, here are some devices for internal structure that may help you:

1. *Start Strong*. When presenting your three main supporting ideas in the body of the speech, place the strongest point first, the next strongest at the end and bury the weakest ones in the middle. Audiences tend to remember whatever is said first or last.

2. *Enumerate*. Use numbers to let the audience keep track of where you are: first, second or first, next, etc. Numbers provide instant order and act as a tracking device for an audience which is always more content to know precisely where they are on their journey through a speech.

3. *Use Transitions*. Give the audience sign-posts along the speech journey before you take a turn in the road. Where possible,

place transitions at the beginning of
sentences so listeners will get an early
warning. Instead of saying, "The country is
in danger of pollution, however." Try this
form, "However, the country is in danger."
The following words will help the audience
anticipate your new directions:

Speech Transitions

Relationship to Establish	Transition Words to Use
addition	also, and, moreover, further, similarly, likewise
comparison	in the same way, likewise
contrast/opposition	but, however, on the other hand, yet
cause and effect	as a result, thus, therefore, hence
time and/or space	above, around, earlier, soon, then
summary	at last, finally, in conclusion, to summarize

4. ***Be Consistent***. Use a consistent system to order your outline. The following lettering-numbering-and-indenting system represents a widely accepted hierarchy for any outline:

    I. Outline Order
        A. Main Idea
            1. Subheading
            2. Subheading
                a) xxxx
                b) yyyy
                    (1) etc.
                    (2) etc.
  II.

5. ***Keep Parallel Structure***. To show equivalent weight and importance in an outline, maintain a structure that is grammatically parallel. For example:

  II. Ways to Keep in Shape
        A. Bicycl*ing*
        B. Runn*ing*
        C. Walk*ing*

6. ***Maintain Proportion***. All too often more space is allotted to a particular idea in the outline than its relative weight to the overall speech. Further, segments of the speech

should be in proportion to their importance. For example, the introduction should be approximately 15% of the entire outline or draft. Thus, if you have a 10-page draft, the introduction should be about one and one-half pages long. The conclusion should not be more than about one page long (10% of the outline or draft). Thus, the body of the speech should be about seven and one-half pages; each section in the body would be approximately two and one-half pages. Therefore, if you find one section exceptionally long or short, you'll need to evaluate it more closely. Indeed, you may have a lopsided speech. The easiest way to check the proportion of the speech is to lay it out sequentially on a table or on the floor (if the table is not long enough to accommodate it). By viewing it laid out end to end, you will be able to easily count pages and check proportion.

THE FIFTH RULE:

Pretest Your Outline

Would you buy a car without taking a test drive or buy a suit without trying it on? Most people pretest whatever is important to them. What could be more important than expressing your ideas in public? Ironically, few public speakers ever pretest their material before presenting it before the intended audience. Think of it—the first time you find out whether your ideas will fly or not is before the very audience you intend to impress. Very risky business.

To ensure that your speech will get the reception you desire, take a page out of your marketing manager's manual and develop a pilot study or a test group. Consider this: Would any self-respecting company introduce a new product without doing some pre-evaluation or test marketing? Hardly—the cost of failure is too high. Before any company produces a million widgits, it will always want to know what the likely reception will be by pre-testing the product on a sample group which is representative of the entire intended market.

There are sophisticated and often times consuming methods to select representative samples and conduct pretests or pilot studies. However, as a speaker, you can pretest your speech simply, yet effectively, by using a response group. This chapter will discuss what a response group does. It will then discuss other editing options such as editing by individuals, subject-matter experts and finally, self-editing techniques.

SPEECH RESPONSE GROUPS

To get reactions to your speech, form your own mini-audience: A speech response group. Members can be friends, coworkers, family — anyone who will take the time to read and respond honestly to your speech. It's critical at various stages of the speechwriting process to have independent, outside reaction to your speech. Often as the author, you'll be much too close and too invested in your work to be objective. Therefore, to get an honest assessment, you'll need to use a test group. Further, consider also that all brains are not all wired the same way. Some people are exceptional with broad sweeping concepts (paint with a broad brush) and others are fact-based, detail people. Both are necessary to make a speech truly effective because every audience will be composed of both types. Thus, by having several others respond to your speech, preferably in a group meeting, you're more likely to get the view you may be missing. In fact, the closer your speech response group matches the audience in personality, education, experience—the more precise their response will match that of the intended audience.

How large should the group be? Three to five people is ideal. Fewer than three seriously limits your ability to discover trends and problems in your speech. However, more than five people in a group setting makes it difficult to set up or control a meeting.

With several responses, you, as the author, can take advantage of triangulation: observing where three people point out the same strengths or weaknesses. You can bet that if three people independently find something is strong or weak in your speech that it accurately reflects what a larger audience would also pick out.

GROUP SPEECHWRITING CONFERENCE

To make the group speechwriting conference work the way it should, you'll need to follow a few simple but necessary rules:

1. Ensure that all members of the group have sufficient time to read and edit the draft before the meeting.

2. Conduct the meeting with all members present in a setting away from phones and outside disturbances.

3. Tape record the entire session. By recording the session, the author will be able to capture the offhand, but most useful comments as well as capture the valuable inter- action that takes place when a group gets together to discuss a common topic.

4. Designate someone other than the author to conduct the meeting—to act as a monitor.

5. Begin by having the author discuss what seemed to work well in the speech. Begin- ning on a positive note reduces author anxiety and increases receptivity to input.

6. Ask the group to comment on what things worked well for them. Honest compliments work well to reduce author anxiety.

7. Ask the author to discuss where he had trouble in the speech.

8. Have the response group members com- ment on where they had trouble with the speech.

9. Give the author the edited speech copies and the tape to use in revision.

EDITING ONE-ON-ONE

Often you may have little or no time to schedule a speechwriting response group. The next best thing is to get someone whose judgment you trust to edit the draft and sit down to discuss it with you. To get effective feedback and to minimize author defensiveness and anxiety, ask your critic to follow a simple formula: The P–Q–P System: Praise–Questions–Polish.

Have her begin by telling you what works well: praise. She should be specific with praise and not gratuitous. Forget those sweeping warm fuzzies that are meaningless, like, "I found the piece most enjoyable and interesting." Rather, she should be specific, "I was impressed with the scientific data that you reported on page 6 concerning the impact of rain forests on the ozone layer." It's rather obvious from this last comment that the reader has read and closely analyzed the speech. Indeed, a compliment from a knowledgeable person is much more believable.

Your critic should begin with praise because it is the least intrusive comment that one can make on a personal level. Remember that in order to ever get to the deepest level of criticism, you must first take the least intrusive steps to "earn the right" to criticize. Just think about it. Would you walk up to a stranger in the street and give her feedback about how her dress could be better coordinated with the rest of her outfit? Hardly. You may tell a friend whose trust you have earned over the years, but even that is difficult. So, too, in the editing process, one needs to set up a gradual trust relationship. This is done by beginning with praise.

Following that step, your friend should do the next least intrusive thing: Ask questions. "I was not sure what you were trying to say in this sentence. What exactly do you mean when you say 'to minimize the impact of contraintuitive thinking'?" Merely asking the quesiton usually draws enough attention to the obviously confusing parts of the speech that you, as the author, will often want to correct immediately. Questions are nonjudgmental and, therefore, don't intrude on the author—even though they are a step closer toward direct editing.

Finally, by now your (the author's) natural anxiety is reduced and your critic has earned the right to be more direct in her editing. Now she may offer direct polish—things that need to be done to make the draft stronger. Even so, she should use language that is more suggestive than directive until she sees how you (the author) are taking her comments. For example, she might begin by saying, "You might want to consider a change..." or, "What do you think about substituting..." Remember that all of us are protective of our creations whether it be children or pieces of writing. However, the practice of editing or correction is still the same—we must earn the right to be critical before we plow ahead into the process.

For most people this is not a natural process. Most have had the "authority—red-pencil" model to copy. Most authorities/teachers begin with spelling errors, awkward sentences and things that need to be corrected to "make it perfect." Thus, the first response most authors get from most people is what was wrong—and at a most vulnerable time in the creative writing process. Take time to indoctrinate your responder about the P–Q–P System, especially if you intend to have an ongoing editing relationship with her or him. It will make a tremendous difference in the productivity of your relationship and of your writing.

SUBJECT-MATTER EXPERTS

Besides making sure that the speech makes sense and is well written, you will also want to make sure that it is substantively correct. Are your facts and concepts about the rain forest, for example, correct? The quickest and most reliable way to ensure substantive correctness is to ask experts on the topic—subject-matter experts—to review your draft outline.

Do you want experts to check the grammar, syntax and spelling of your outline? No. First, because it would bog them down by taking too long—wasting valuable time that could be used checking substance. Someone else can handle the editorial side later. Second, the subject-matter experts are experts in their field, not English. They may be totally incapable of any reliable editing. And besides, that's not why you brought your draft to them. Stick with their expertise to get the most out of the review. And let them know up front that you

don't want them to edit—only to check for
substantive accuracy.

SELF-EDITING

Perhaps the fastest but most difficult editing task you can perform is self-editing.
Because you, as an author, are so close to your
own speech, it's difficult to get far enough
away to become objective. But the reality of
the workplace is that often you don't have
someone handy to respond or circumstances
won't permit outside response. So, you only
have yourself to rely on for editing. Here are
some tips to help you get enough distance to
be a more objective self-editor:

1. ***Put Your Writing Away.*** Even if it's only
   long enough to go out and have lunch,
   you'll be surprised how letting the ink cool
   provides you with a more objective eye.
   Ideally, if you can let a day or two pass,
   you will be much more objective—time
   lapse and objectivity are directly related.

2. ***Read Your Speech Aloud.*** The ear seems to
   have more objectivity than the eye—
   especially with speeches, which are ultimately intended for the ear. You will liter-
   ally "hear" the excellent parts and the

trouble spots alike as you read your speech aloud.

3. ***Tape Record Your Reading Aloud.*** Then play the tape back. Since few of us think that tape recordings "sound like us," the tape has the same effect as having someone else read your speech aloud.

4. ***Edit from Double- or Triple-Spaced Copy.*** Such spacing invites editing. Single-spaced drafts actually prohibit editing.

5. ***Edit at Your Sharpest Time of Day.*** If you are a morning person, edit in the morning. If your best time is at midnight, edit then. You know when you are sharpest.

6. ***Do Not Edit with a Red Pen or Pencil.*** Red means failure and because it dredges up painful memories of Miss Crabtree in the 5th grade who took off three points for every misspelled word and who circled them with a big red circle. So, don't use red. This goes for self-editing and especially if you edit someone else's work.

   Use a blue pencil. Most professional editors use erasable blue pencil, which is available at most stationery stores. Blue makes it easy to find your corrections without subconsciously upsetting yourself or anyone you might be editing.

Editing, whether by using a group, a friend or yourself, is a necessary but often painful part of the composing process. However, editing doesn't have to be so difficult if you remember the P–Q–P System and a few of the tips mentioned in this chapter. Always remember that every creation can be improved by editing, and the more objective that editing, the more likely it will help improve your final product.

THE SIXTH RULE:

Write Out the Speech Draft

With the feedback on your outline from your speech response group, you are ready to write the draft. Whether you decide ultimately to use a speaking outline or a full-text speech draft, you should write and polish your draft as if it were going into the history books. Why? Because it just might, and it also forces you to thoroughly formulate your ideas by making you write them down for you and others to edit.

Further, when very important speeches, such as policy speeches or high-impact speeches are given, you will want the record to be absolutely correct. Indeed, the further up the corporate ladder you climb, the more important it is to be correct; thus, there is increasing need to use a draft or at least have one prepared for dissemination following your speech.

Therefore, this chapter will focus on preparing a full-text, manuscript speech draft. First, it will discuss how to write the draft, then it will provide speechwriting tips and finally address how to format a manuscript.

WRITING THE DRAFT

If you had to pick a stalling point in most manuscript speeches, it would have to come at the initial drafting stage. Overcoming inertia is very difficult. Even with a revised outline in hand, many people just cannot get started, and consequently freeze with writer's block—that inability to move the pen across the paper or to punch a key on a computer.

Fortunately, there are a couple of fail-safe methods for moving the ideas in your mind and on an outline to the draft stage. The two methods that this chapter will deal with are freewriting (which was discussed briefly in Chapter 3) and freespeaking. Both techniques are quick, simple and as nonthreatening as you could imagine.

Freewriting

Although freewriting was addressed in an earlier chapter, it's worth revisiting here because it is so important. Remember, it's just like writing to a friend. Don't worry about correct spelling or grammar usage. Just put pen or pencil to paper or pound out words on your word processor; let the words fly and don't look back. Though it will be difficult at first to let obvious errors slip by, resist the temptation to correct—it will ultimately be faster to let them stand and correct them later. Certainly, use the outline to prompt your thoughts. If you generally follow the outline, revisions will be much easier later. However, don't be concerned if your thoughts take you away from the outline—it's only a guide to your writing, not a law that you must follow.

The rules for freewriting are simple:

1. Choose your favorite pen, pencil, computer, paper, chair and place to write—they all make a difference.

2. Imagine that you're writing to a good friend—one who knows you can't spell perfectly and who knows that your grammar sometimes falters.

3. Write to someone you trust, such as a close friend.

4. Don't stop until you've written all you know about the topic.

5. Remember not to slow down to correct errors.

6. Use your outline only as a guide.

Freespeaking

Have you ever heard anyone say, "Oh, I'm just thinking out loud." Well, freespeaking takes advantage of a natural instinct for some: talking to themselves.

This technique uses the strongly developed oral skills that most people naturally have to formulate the basis for a written draft. The disadvantage of the technique is that spoken drafts often contain a great deal of repetition and "flab" that you will want to delete eventually.

In a sense, freespeaking is like dictation, but it flows more freely. To freespeak you need a tape recorder, and you need to pretend that you're talking to someone—a specific audience, a trusted friend. Although the initial words may be awkward, after a few minutes words will flow easily. Keep your tone conversational, and the words will come naturally.

You should freespeak until you finish your thoughts on the topic. As with freewriting, use your outline as a structural guide to address your topic. However, be prepared to take detours along the way and to make major revisions. Remember this is only a rough draft.

The following are the basic steps in free-speaking:

1. Set up a tape recorder in a quiet room.

2. Assume a trusted friend is your audience.

3. Use your outline as a guide.

4. Speak freely in a conversational way.

5. Transcribe your recording using double spacing to prepare the draft for revisions.

Freespeaking and freewriting are like priming a pump: they get the ideas flowing. With those ideas comes language. By selecting a nonthreatening audience, thinking and expressing your thoughts become easier and quicker. Both techniques unleash the power of your brain by helping to remove your writing anxiety. If you want to practice freewriting, sit down and write letters to two or three friends; the technique is that simple. If you want to practice freespeaking, talk to yourself out loud about anything. Now how difficult can that be!

SPEECHWRITING TIPS

When you begin to refine your freewriting or freespeaking, you should be aware of some tricks of the speechwriting trade that will help

your final draft read well. What follows are just
a few basic tips that might help you:

1. *Use Simple Words.* Don't try to impress
   your audience with how many long words
   you know. The objective of effective
   communication is to convey your thoughts
   as clearly as you can; so, avoid the
   temptation.

   Stuffy: When a populace purloins,
                   restitution must be added.

   Clear: When people steal, they must
                   repay.

2. *Use Concrete Language.* Avoid fuzzy or
   hazy generalizations. Instead, paint a clear
   picture for the audience. Remember that
   the picture you create in words is the only
   one they will "see."

   Hazy: My supervisor possesses the
                   requisite skills to navigate a
                   vehicle with dexterity in con-
                   gested traffic.

   Clear: My boss drives a car through
                   heavy traffic with the ease and
                   skill of a race car driver.

3. ***Use Strong Verbs.*** Verbs are the lifeblood of any sentence. Avoid the verb "is" in any of its forms and watch the sentence come alive:

   Dull: We were so pleased that Congress took the appropriate action when it voted for the new conservation bill.

   Alive: We screamed "Hooray" at the top of our lungs after Congress passed the new conservation bill.

4. ***Use Short Sentences.*** Remember that you will have to "breathe" any sentence you write. Sentences over 20 words long (about two to three typewritten lines) tend to be difficult to say in one breath. Test your draft out loud and see. If a sentence runs longer than one breath, add some places along the way to breathe.

   Breathless: We think of the pollution in the air as a great, horrific cloud that looms overhead like some pall which traps the stale, dead air over us like a blanket smothering our every breath as we wait for someone of courage to tear it off and save us from our own doing.

Air at last: Pollution is like a horrific cloud looming overhead which traps the stale, dead air over us like a poisonous blanket. As we smother under it, we wait for someone of courage to tear it off and save us from our own doing.

5. *Vary Sentence Lengths.* Sentences should vary. Some may be short like the first two in this paragraph and others longer like this one, which is intended to make the point that not all need to be short to be effective. In fact, by placing short and long sentences side-by-side, you can add emphasis.

6. *Avoid Shifts in Number, Tense, Gender or Subject.*

   Number: Subjects should always match their verbs and pronouns.

   Mixed: The Representative votes his conscience or at least they should.

   Clear: Representatives vote their consciences or at least they should.

Tense: Avoid shifting verb tense to keep things clear.

Untimely: The lobbyist viewed the activities of the House and later registers his complaint to no avail.

On time: The lobbyist viewed the activities of the House and registered his complaint to no avail.

Gender: Be careful to avoid gender-biased words in any speech. Especially avoid titles that immediately are perceived as sexist.

Biased: The policeman escorted the boisterous man from the Senate gallery.

Unbiased: The police officer escorted the boisterous man from the Senate gallery.

Subject: Avoid moving from the active to the passive voice in the same sentence.

Mixed: The writer finished her rough draft and then it was revised.

Clear: The writer finished her rough draft and then revised it.

7. **_Tell Stories._** Everyone loves stories. From the time you were a child, people told stories to get attention and to illustrate points. Take advantage of a cultural practice and begin by saying, "Let me tell you a story . . ." You'll be amazed at the responsiveness of your audience.

8. **_Use "Because" When Giving Reasons._** Research in persuasion has shown that the word "because" is a naturally persuasive trigger word for most people. When they hear it, they are often convinced by what follows because they expect and often accept what follows as reason for the condition.

Unclear:	He would not move from his position since he was not sure it was in his constituency's best interest.
Clearer:	He would not move from his position because he was not sure it was in his constituency's best interest.

9. **_Put Style in Your Speech._** Try some of these devices to give life to your speech:

- **Simile** — a direct comparison of two similar things: "Her voice was like a whisper from a dying woman."

- **Metaphor** — an implied comparison: "His words cut the air until it almost bled."

- **Antithesis** — parallel words, phrases or sentences with opposing ideas: "Let us work to live. But never live to work."

- **Amplification** — reinforcement or enlarging on a statement or declaration: "Let us move forward, advance and never quit what we have begun this day."

- **Alliteration** — repetition of initial sounds: "The people proudly praised the work of a conscientious Congress."

- **Assonance** — similar sounding vowels: "Might should never make right."

- Use **repetition** for emphasis: "We will fight. We will work. We will win."

- **Rhetorical** questions — questions to be answered only in the audience's mind: "Ask yourselves: What would I have done in a similar situation?"

- Use **fragments** for emphasis: "How long would it take? A day? A week? A month?"

FORMATTING A MANUSCRIPT SPEECH

The physical appearance of the manuscript is most important to the speaker. A poorly formatted speech throws roadblocks in front of the speaker. Fortunately, there are some ways to overcome these pitfalls.

1. *Use Large Fonts.* Computers come equipped with a variety of type fonts that are larger and easier to read. The extra size also makes for shorter, more manageable eye sweeps across the page. You absorb the material quicker, with less eye strain, and you can give the audience more eye contact because your eyes are not riveted on tiny print. In the absence of an oversized font, you might consider using copying machines that have built-in enlargers. Even though enlarged copies tend to be more grainy, it's a fair trade-off.

2. ***Triple Space the Draft.*** Triple spacing allows the eye to track the words more readily. You also can easily insert last-minute details and corrections, and you are less likely to lose your place, or worse yet, skip a line or two as you read. With ample space between lines, you can effortlessly keep a finger or eye on your lines as a quick reference point.

3. ***Use Ample Margins.*** When writing drafts, use at least 1- to 2-inch margins to shorten the length of the line. Long lines make eye sweeps more difficult and force you to look at the draft rather than at the audience—a habit that often alienates them.

4. ***Provide Eye Breaks.*** Even if your speech contains relatively short sentences, inserting eye breaks will allow you to look at the audience more. Periods at the end of the sentences offer a natural stopping point. Commas within the draft provide a breather; dashes (—) allow you to pause even more; and a paragraph break gives you time to look up and around at the audience.

5. ***Keep Paragraphs Short.*** As mentioned, the end of a paragraph provides opportunity for you to make quality eye contact with your audience. To determine if you have enough paragraphs, scan each page. If you don't have a single paragraph on a page, you need to find a place for a break in the text. From a purely editorial standpoint, the chances are unusually high that with no paragraph break in a single page, you will need to insert one to have the text make sense and flow better.

   As a general guideline, use three to five sentences in a paragraph. Fewer sentences may produce an underdeveloped paragraph; more sentences, an overly complex one.

6. ***Add Parenthetical Directions to Yourself in Brackets.*** It's one thing to write a speech in the quiet of your home or office, but quite another to deliver that speech under the bright lights with hundreds of people watching you. Adrenaline flow may cause you to miss the opportunities to pause at the right time. Without realizing it, you may simply barrel along like a sprinter heading for the finish line.

Parenthetical directions placed in brackets can help break this impulse and many others. Use brackets liberally to give yourself stage directions like: [Smile!] or [Pause]. Each direction will help you punctuate the reading of your text with powerful nonverbal communication. You can also use parenthetical notes to show phonetic spelling of names and words and to add last minute notes that you think of just before you rise to the podium. Maybe it will be something that the previous speaker says or a passing thought, but by marking it down, you know you will have it if you need it later.

7. ***Have Your Response Group Review the Speech.*** As with the speech outline, getting your response group's reaction to the draft is critical. Pretesting will save you from some most embarrassing moments. Don't forget a last review by a subject-matter expert just to make sure your information is correct.

Speechwriting with style is an art, and like any art it requires both technique and practice. Understanding how to get your ideas on paper quickly, how to introduce stylistic devices to

your draft and how to format the manuscript
will make all the difference between the failure
and success of your speech.

THE SEVENTH RULE:

Make Your Presentation

With your draft in hand, you must now turn to the task of making your presentation. In fact, delivery may be more important than content; that is, how you deliver your speech may be actually more memorable than what you say. Indeed, it's not uncommon for people to say of a speaker, "I'm not exactly sure what he said, but the way he said it was so good." What accounts for such statements is the effective use of nonverbal communication by public speakers.

Research estimates indicate that nonverbal communication accounts for between 65% and 93% of our personal communication. Such nonverbals as eye contact, movement, gestures and sound quality all impact the message we project.

This chapter will first discuss two types of public speaking delivery options: the extemporaneous speech and the manuscript or full-text speech. It will then cover the major nonverbal techniques used in public speaking such as eye contact, gestures, movement and sound quality.

DELIVERY OPTIONS

When you commit to speak to a particular group, you will need to decide on what type of delivery method you should best employ: extemporaneous or manuscript speech delivery. Let's take a moment to define both and then look at each in more depth.

The Extemporaneous Speech

The extemporaneous speech is often misunderstood for impromptu speech (often called "winging it"). There is a vast difference between the (prepared) extemporaneous speech and off-the-cuff impromptu remarks. First, to be a good extemporaneous speaker requires hours of practice for a particular speech, even for the most accomplished speaker. Extemporaneous speakers work from keyword notes and speaking outlines, not full-text drafts. Impromptu speakers, on the other hand, work by the seat of their pants. While this technique can be developed for those rare occasions on which you might get called upon to speak without any preparation, it's far better to concentrate your efforts on developing planned, extemporaneous speeches.

To deliver an extemporaneous speech, you will need to develop a keyword list which will cue you to remember significant bits of information and keep you on track throughout your speech. To help you develop a keyword list, read the manuscript you have written (regardless of what delivery system you'll be using) and highlight the keywords. Now write down the keywords in order of highlighting and you'll have the basis for your list. Don't be afraid to revise your list. Nothing is sacred. The purpose of the list is to help you remember.

Rehearsal, while important for any delivery style you choose, is of *absolute importance* in the extemporaneous speech precisely because all the data is not written down. In fact, the degree of preparation for this type of speech is one factor to consider when choosing your delivery option. So, when might you use an extemporaneous speech?

- When you want to impress an audience with how much you know—your command of a topic. By having to rely minimally on notes, you will duly impress any audience.

- When you want to strike a personal bond with an audience. Such speeches allow maximum eye contact and, thus, speaker credibility.

- When you want to appear to be dynamic. Again, mastery of your topic allows you to vary from notes, move around more, be more natural and therefore appear more dynamic and powerful.

What are the drawbacks; why wouldn't everyone use such a speech? It takes a lot of time to master any topic and then to prepare such a speech.

So, what's a good alternative? A manuscript speech.

The Manuscript Speech

The manuscript or full-text speech provides an option particularly for the public speaker who considers accuracy, time, technical proficiency and a manuscript for the record a must. Used by presidents, CEOs and government leaders as a mainstay, the manuscript speech is worth its weight in gold to most public speakers.

Several tips on how to prepare the manuscript speech were provided in the previous chapter; therefore, this segment will concentrate on how to deliver from a manuscript.

- **Read Slowly.** Perhaps the greatest single mistake that most speakers make is to read too quickly. What seems like an hour to you, as the speaker, may be a second or two in reality because your adrenaline speeds up time. Take a hint from most track coaches to runners: don't sprint when you should pace yourself.

- **Score Your Draft.** Just like a symphony conductor, mark special directions on the draft and follow them. To emphasize words, highlight them with see-through markers. Use diagonal slash marks to help slow you down when you want to emphasize a point, a word or an emotional moment.

- **Use Systematic Eye Contact.** Maintaining eye contact presents one great difficulty with a manuscript speech, and you know by now how important that is to a presentation. But by developing a system of eye contact while reading a manuscript speech, you can overcome some of the problem. One method is to always begin by looking down at the draft, picking up the first portion of the sentence, then looking back up at the audience and delivering only when you are looking at them. Then, at the appropriate punctuation point (pause mark) you dip your head down again to pick up the words, then bring the head back up for delivery. To keep your place as you read, keep one index finger on the text, usually the nondominant index finger, which allows for gesturing with the dominant hand. This method for manuscript delivery ensures maximum eye contact. It requires lots of preparation, short sentences and a slowed down delivery pace.

As an alternative reading style, try the up-down-up technique. Begin by delivering the first part of the sentence with eyes on the audience and then go back to the text for the middle of the sentence, which is read with eyes on the text. When you get to the end of the sentence or paragraph, come up for delivery with eyes squarely on the audience. This up-down-up technique must be practiced but is generally easier than the first method, though not quite as effective. Here are some additional tips to assist you:

- **_Keep Eyes Up When You Shift Pages._** When
  you are about to finish a page and move to
  the next one, subtly move the page to your
  left or right so you can see both that page
  and the next one side by side. If you always
  end each page with at least a period, you
  will be able to make this shift as you deliver
  your last line with your eyes on the
  audience. Therefore, the shift is imper-
  ceptible by the audience.

- **_Carry Your Speech in a File Folder._** Not only
  does this keep your speech from getting
  lost, soiled or crumpled, but it also serves
  as your podium if you are ever called to
  speak without a podium. By having a stiff-
  backed file folder you can deliver a speech
  from a solitary standing position without
  fear that the paper will be shaking in your
  hand because of the adrenaline that's
  pumping.

- **_Rehearse Out Loud._** Rehearsal builds
  confidence; so, rehearse as much as you
  can. Of course, you will always have the
  comfort of a draft if you have little or no
  time to rehearse. That's the value of a
  draft.

NONVERBALS

Anyone who has ever seen a mime perform knows the power of nonverbal communication. Children and animals know just by the tone of the adult voice whether to come close or stay away. A cold-eyed stare by a parent can silence a child who is acting up. And the excited wave of someone greeting a friend at an airport or bus station has unmistakable meaning. So often, nothing need be said and still communication is loud and clear. As a speaker you must master the use of nonverbals to communicate effectively. Let's review some of the most important nonverbals you should use in your speech.

Eye Contact

The single most important nonverbal in our society is eye contact. It gets drummed in from an early age, "Look me in the eye and tell me the truth." Indeed, eye contact is strongly associated with telling the truth; thus, speaker credibility depends largely on eye contact alone. First, strong eye contact will develop a strong sense of believability in the speaker—as someone to trust. Second, eye contact increases the audience's level of comprehension which further adds to speaker acceptance.

Beyond establishing speaker credibility and increasing audience comprehension, eye contact provides speakers with a most important ingredient to any speech: feedback. As a speaker you can gauge how you're doing based on what your eyes tell you—if you have good eye contact. For instance, if you are delivering a speech, and you look out at everyone riveted on you, you're doing well. They're impressed, intent and eager to hear what you're telling them. If you look closer and see that 20 out of 25 have their arms crossed and eyebrows furrowed, now you know that while they may be impressed, intent and eager—they may be ready to lynch you! Arms crossed are a dead giveaway that people are not buying your message. But how would you even know what they were thinking if you didn't ever look. Eye contact takes care of that by providing feedback. Of course, if you get good feedback, continue to do what you're doing. If you get negative feedback, change direction—try a different approach.

There are two types of eye contact depending on the audience size and whether you're delivering from a text or notes. First, consider sweeping eye contact for large audiences or when you read a manuscript speech. Because your eye contact is necessarily limited by both factors, you need to use a strategy to ensure full coverage with limited contact. Simply divide the audience into thirds: left, middle and right. Each time you pick up your head, systematically address a particular third of the audience. Move systematically and slowly from the left, to the middle, to the right, then back to the middle and so on. By using this method, you give everyone in the audience an equal share of your understandably limited time.

The second type of eye contact is called individual eye contact. The most personal and powerful type of eye contact, you should use this type in smaller groups (50 people or less). It creates very high levels of speaker credibility, and is not any different than the eye contact you employ in your day-to-day social encounters. Just think of what you do when you're speaking to two or three people in a social setting, and you'll have a perfect model for individual eye contact. You look at whomever you're talking to at the moment.

Simple, but powerful—especially in a speech context—this method works. As you are speaking, lock on to a particular individual for two or three seconds and then move on to the next person until you have individually engaged every person in the room. Then start over by systematically re-engaging each one again and again. Each time you lock on to a member of the audience, you establish a personal bond of trust and credibility, so important to a public speaker.

What should you look out for with respect to eye contact?

- ■ *Avoid Darting Your Eyes Back and Forth.* You'll look more like a scared rabbit than a confident orator.

- ■ *Don't Wear Tinted Glasses or Any at All If You Don't Need to.* With tints and glass glare, it's difficult for people to see your eyes no matter how hard they or you try.

- ■ *Try Not to Stare at Any One Person Too Long.* There is a tendency to look at particularly attractive, attentive or disruptive people in the audience. Treat them all the same.

Gestures

We gesture every day to hail a cab, wave goodbye, point at signs and punctuate our daily speech. In fact, if you were to videotape a normal conversation between two people, you would probably have a perfect model for learning how to use gestures in public speaking. For indeed, if public speaking is done well, it looks like an extended conversation with friends; gestures are relaxed and natural.

Gestures allow the audience's brains to process information on an additional channel and, therefore, comprehend better. First, the brain operates on the voice or language channel and processes the words that you, the speaker, use. Second, the brain operates on the visual channel and by viewing gestures "sees" what you're saying. Good speakers actually draw pictures naturally for audiences.

Gestures can show proportion, direction, height, width, flow—all with the sweep of your hands. You can use one or both hands. You can alternate them. It's your choice. The rule is simple: Do whatever you would in a normal conversation with two or three people. The only difference is that the larger the audience, the more you have to enlarge or amplify your gestures so that people in the back can see them. Though amplifying gestures to fit the size of the crowd may come naturally to most people you need to be reminded of it occasionally. Also consider the following tips about gestures:

- *Avoid Stuffing Your Hands in Your Pockets.* It's fine to occasionally put hands in pockets but be conscious not to leave them there because your gestures will become completely, though unconsciously, inhibited.

- *Keep Your Hands in a Steepling Position in Front of You.* The steepling position looks like you are praying. The finger tips from both hands are gently pressed together, thus forming a church steeple. By using this technique, you make your hands available for gesturing. Now instead of having them locked in your pockets, you have them cocked and ready for action. As you begin to relax, you will increase your gestures exponentially.

- *Hold Your Notes in Your Non-dominant Hand.* The non-dominant hand is the one opposite from the one you write with. By keeping your notes in that hand you'll have one hand free to gesture, and you will prevent yourself from waving your notes around wildly and distracting your audience.

Movement

Consider this simple equation: Space = Relationships. Now think about how you move to maintain space in your everyday life. You move close to someone you like and away from people you don't like or don't know. Therefore, movement can change your relationship to people with subtle efforts on your part as a public speaker. Most speakers maintain a very formal distance from their audiences and never take advantage of this nonverbal powerhouse: movement.

But you can. By simply moving toward a portion of the audience you can establish a new, more intimate relationship with them. By moving back to the podium you can get more information from your notes and then approach yet another part of the audience — all the time engaging them in natural, personal speech.

Besides building relationships, movement can perform another important function for the careful public speaker: Attracting attention. Consider the last time someone waved a hand or threw a ball in your presence. Your eye naturally tracked the moving object. So it is with the public speakers who move meaning-fully. To do so you must move with your eyes on the audience, lest you look like a parent pacing and staring at the floor while waiting for a teenager to return home late from a date. However, methodical movement both from side to side and to and from the audience makes speakers "trackable" and attracts audience attention. Even when locked into a podium and public address system, the speaker can consciously shift toward one side of the podium or the other and lean in or back away from the podium. It is surprising what impact such subtle shifts make to an audience.

Sound Quality

Speeches are meant to be heard; therefore, sound is a most important factor in the nonver-bal equation. We have all suffered through a monotoned teacher, a speaker or a pastor. Indeed, an uninflected voice will send even the most ardent listener to dreamland. To preclude putting the audience to sleep, public speakers should employ three aspects of sound: tone, tempo and volume.

- **Tone** is the inflection you put in your
  voice—the quality of the sound that you
  give a word. Depending on the "spin" you
  put on a word, you can convey entirely
  separate meanings. Consider the word
  "*yes*." There's the kind of enthusiastic
  "yes" that a new employee uses who is
  excited to do a great job. Then there is the
  dragged out, almost painful "Y-E-S" of a
  child finally agreeing, after much debate, to
  clean her messy room. Yes, there are all
  kinds of ways to give additional meaning to
  words just based on the tone you give
  them. As a public speaker, if you infuse
  your speech with enthusiasm and inflection,
  the audience will pick up your eagerness.
  On the other hand, if you slip into a monotoned, ho-hum delivery you can probably
  guess their corresponding response.

- **Tempo** adds another dimension to sound.
  Just as in music, tempo can greatly affect
  the quality and impact of your spoken
  words. Most people speak publicly at 125
  words per minute, but the ear can absorb
  easily at 200 or more words per minute—
  leaving a gap that is often used by listeners
  for daydreaming. The solution: Vary the
  tempo. Speak quickly during certain

portions of your speech for emphasis and slow way down below 100 words per minute for emphasis in other sections. Both slow and fast shifts attract attention; they indicate that you are making a point and perk up even the sleepiest listener.

- **Volume** is the last in the dynamic sound trio. Volume can run the range from soft to loud. And just as no audience appreciates a speaker who whispers constantly, neither do they want a screamer either. Consider again personal conversation that you can always use as a model for self-teaching about public speaking. No conversation has only one volume to it. If you don't believe it, turn on a tape recorder one day in your office and listen to the rich variety of not only tone, tempo, but also volume in even the most routine conversations. In public speaking, volume helps to underscore certain important words, phrases or sentences of your speech because increased or varied volume perks up the audience's attention by saying subtly to them, "Hey, now! You might want to listen carefully to what I'm saying."

THE EIGHTH RULE:

*Be Prepared
for Anything*

Many people have heard of Murphy's Law, but all public speakers have experienced it: "If anything can go wrong, it probably will." Despite what you may have thought, the size of the audience, the size of the room, the mood of the people, the lighting—you name it— something will be much different than you expected. Knowing how to deal with unexpected problems will not eliminate them, but will help you adjust to them. Of course, to avoid the big problems, anticipate and prepare for them.

This chapter will discuss the preparation cycle that you should go through to get ready for your speech, and then it will deal with several special situations in which speakers may find themselves.

PREPARATION: THE KEY

Remember the Boy Scout motto: "Always be prepared." All public speakers should also have that same motto. Much like the pro golfer who steps up to the tee and blasts the ball hundreds of yards straight down the fairway with almost no perceptible effort, a good speaker makes it look easy. That's the trick. However, like the golfer who practices for hours on end, you too must put in practice time—to make it *look* easy. Indeed, making anything look easy means tough, grueling practice that is anything but easy. So, let's look at a regimen of training preparation to help you get your speech game into shape for the big day when you play it out in front of real, live fans.

BEFORE SPEECH DAY

Like any athlete, your road to success begins with the first day of practice—long before speech day. As was mentioned previously in this book ("The Second Rule"), you should conduct exhaustive analysis of the audience, occasion and your objective. While there is no need to describe that process again in detail, you must be aware that accurate analysis can eliminate most of your problems. But, let's take a look at those special practice drills that can give you a leg up on your speech—that can make your speech not just good but exceptional.

- **Study the Audience, Occasion and Location.** Sure, you have already done the analysis, but go back over it until you know it like the back of your hand. Have as absolutely clear a picture of the entire situation as you can have. However, be ready to revise it as new information comes your way.

- **Read the Daily News.** A week and just before (a day or two) your speech, be sure to check the papers, especially the local periodicals about your group. Certainly if you have access to the Internet or *Lexus/Nexus* (a computerized databank of up-to-date news clips) you should employ it. Also check at your local library. Many now have on-line computer databanks which they will run for a nominal fee. Such current information can truly make a significant difference.

- **Develop a Game Plan.** Anyone who has watched a professional football game has seen the coach or his assistant toting around a clipboard or a laminated sheet with plays and notes for the game—the game plan. With a familiar game plan in hand you will be amazed at how much more comfortable you will feel. What is a game plan? It's nothing more than the notes that you'll actually use on speech day. At some time in the preparation process you must come up with your game plan notes so that you know how they feel and look. Never, ever change the game plan—your notes—before the game unless things have radically changed. Just as no athlete should wear new shoes for a game, don't try on any new note system before your game day or you could be asking for problems.

■ **Rehearse Out Loud.** Because you will deliver your speech out loud, you must practice out loud. "You do in a game what you did in practice," is what the old coach says. This could not be truer in the world of public speaking. Find a quiet room, set up a podium or a box on a table if no podium is available. Position three chairs to your front: one on the right, one in the middle and one on the left to represent the audience in three sections. And, of course: practice, practice, practice.

■ **Practice Your Nonverbals.** For your voice, always use a tape recorder. Set the recorder on one of the chairs to hear how you're projecting. Of course, you will probably have a microphone and your voice will be amplified, but you can be sure that if a recorder in a chair a few feet away does not pick up your voice clearly, you will have problems with voice projection regardless of how much amplification you have.

For your other nonverbals use a video recorder. If you or your company do not own one, they are inexpensive to rent from local video stores. They can effectively show you exactly what you look like as you deliver your speech. For most people, it is a bit of a shock to see themselves, but most informative. Look particularly at what you do with your hands; look for habitually annoying traits like shifting back and forth from one foot to another; look for eye contact and all the other nonverbals so important to a successful presentation.

After you have viewed or listened to your presentation, put the recording away for a day or two. Then play it back when you have allowed time to pass. Remember this important equation: Time = Objectivity. You will see and hear things that you missed on the first review. You can bet on that.

■ ***Get Feedback.*** Ask someone to review your presentation either in person or to review your tape recording. If they use the Praise–Questions–Polish (P–Q–P) method you'll

gain an enormous amount from such a
session. At the very least, have someone
review your final speech draft.

SPEECH DAY

Finally, speech day will come. There are
some tips that might help you do some final
preparation on that day:

- **Arrive Early.** This concept was discussed
  earlier in this book, but it was worth
  repeating. Arrive at the location and check
  the sound system, the lighting, the
  ventilation, potential distractions and the
  need for any equipment or special
  arrangements crucial to your speech.

- **Get Physical.** Get in a physical workout that
  day. Take a walk, run, swim or ride on your
  bike. It will help calm you down. Many
  speakers go for long walks prior to their
  speeches and rehearse the speech mentally
  by envisioning the audience and themselves
  as being very successful as they deliver the
  speech.

- **Carry Your Game Plan with You.** Whether
  you decide to use your draft or key notes,
  don't give them up or place them at the

podium. Take them with you wherever you go. Also check to make sure that they are in order by having large page numbers at the top right-hand corner.

- **Study the Room.** Walk around the room before anyone gets there. Make sure that all in the audience will be able to see your graphics, charts or slides. You can also do this by walking through the room. It will also give you the audience's perspective. Don't be afraid to rearrange either the seating itself or the position of the podium to accommodate the audience.

- **Meet the Audience.** To help you get rid of pre-game jitters, shake hands with the members of the audience as they arrive. Strike up short informal conversations with each and you will be surprised at connections you may have: school, home towns and even mutual friends. This time is well spent because such contact eliminates nervousness by giving you the feeling that you're talking to a group of acquaintances, not strangers. You'll also pick up a lot of valuable tidbits of information to help you personalize your opening comments.

SPECIAL SPEECH SITUATIONS

Despite the best laid plans, unexpected events happen at the last minute, and you will have to adjust. The food may be late, the crowd smaller than expected, the lights dimmer than you wanted. While most annoying situations can be eliminated by preparation, sometimes you just have to be flexible and adjust at the last moment. However, there are a couple of speech situations into which you may be thrust, as a public speaker. Let's review these: the impromptu remarks and the introduction.

Impromptu Remarks

There are those occasions when the emcee says "Maybe our speaker would like to give us a few words on . . ." You have just been asked to give an impromptu speech—the most difficult of all speeches because you have not had time to prepare. Try this approach:

- **Reflect for a Moment.** Audiences can handle it and realize that you're thinking in order to respond thoughtfully, and they will respect that notion.

- **Use Who, What, When, Where, How, and Why.** Asking yourself the basic questions about any topic will give you immediate insight and even a possible structure for your answer.

- **Don't Apologize.** Avoid the inclination to offer excuses for lack of preparation or for being nervous. Most people will never notice unless you call their attention to your shortcomings—so don't. This guideline goes for all speeches: Don't apologize or offer excuses.

- **Repeat the Topic.** This will help stall for time and give you time to think.

- **Make Only One or Two Main Points.** Don't belabor your answer. Keep it simple and direct. Then sit down.

- **Don't Be Afraid to Say You Don't Know.** Better to admit that you are not aware of a situation than to ramble on and prove that you don't know.

THE INTRODUCTION

Though it might not happen often, sometimes you may be asked to introduce another speaker. For whatever reason, if you're placed in this situation, remember a few key tips:

- *Practice Pronouncing the Speaker's Name.*

- *Give the Speaker's Qualifications.*

- *Look at the Speaker* during your introduction, especially when you repeat his or her name.

- *Provide a Simple Structure* such as the speaker's name, qualifications to speak, the topic and its relevance to the audience.

- *Start the Applause* and the audience will follow your lead.

- *Keep It Simple and Dignified* by avoiding corny, sexist or trite expressions such as: "Here's the best guy or gal I know...," "Without further ado...," "The man who needs no introduction..."

THE NINTH RULE:

Answer Questions from the Audience

A famous professional athlete once said, "It ain't over until it's over." This ineloquent, but sage statement captures the *total* speech situation. Many a great speech has disintegrated because the speaker was ill prepared for the questions that followed. Unfortunately, because people tend to remember what they heard first—usually the introduction—and last—usually the response to questions—you must be well prepared for questions that follow your speech. Treat them as the finale of your speech because that's exactly what they are—for better or worse. The purpose of this chapter is to make your speech better, not worse. Again, this is accomplished through preparation and a good strategy. Therefore, this chapter will discuss several rules to help you answer questions concerning your speech.

TIP #1: ANTICIPATE QUESTIONS

Two-thirds of a successful Q-and-A session begins with proper question anticipation. To accomplish this you need to do two things: First, review your audience analysis; second, brainstorm (with others if possible) the kinds of questions you think you might receive.

Because you've already prepared an audience analysis before this point in your speech, that part of question preparation is easy. However, you need to apply your analysis to the basic question: "What would a typical person from this audience ask about my topic?" By analyzing the audience, you raise their natural biases in your mind and thus approach the topic from their point of view. By doing so you will be more likely to encourage the type of questions you are prepared to answer.

But analysis is not enough. You must brainstorm some questions. And while it is possible to raise such questions yourself, it is far more productive and faster to raise those questions in a group setting. Having two or three other people in a room for 15 or 20 minutes brainstorming questions will yield a greater percentage of anticipated questions than you could ever generate in hours by yourself.

To conduct such a meeting, let all participants know the speech topic and generally the nature of the audience. First, give them your outline before the meeting and advise them about what they will be doing in the meeting. Second, make sure that you have

a tape recorder running to capture the
discussion. You will not be able to take notes
as quickly as the questions get asked. Go over
the tape directly after the meeting and draw up
your questions. If you wait too long, you might
lose the momentum.

TIP #2: DEVELOP A STRATEGY TO HANDLE QUESTIONS

The following are a series of hints to help
you handle the general types of questions you
might be asked:

1. ***Have Several Theme Statements Ready.***
   Whenever you go into any Q-and-A session,
   have a few main themes you want to drive
   home. Use the answers to emphasize your
   points. For example, you might want to
   emphasize that among other things, your
   organization has been fair in its handling of
   a particular crisis. Therefore say it: "Once
   again, our company in the absolute interest
   of fair play did the following . . ." Keep
   coming back to your themes time and again
   to ensure that the audience remembers
   them.

2. ***Accept Questions from the Entire Audience.***
Be careful not to get stuck taking questions
from a particular segment of the audience.
All speakers tend to have a side of the
audience, the right or the left, to which
they are partial. It's almost like being right-
or left-handed. Be sure not to short-change
either part of the audience.

3. ***Listen Intently to Questions.***
When asked a question, concentrate on
what the person asks. Repeat the question
in your head and then recite it back to the
questioner—if it's a positive question.

   Positive questions might be defined as
those that do not inherently embarrass the
speaker. An example of a positive question
might be: "What does your company do if
there is an oil spill?" An example of a negative question might be; "Why don't you
guys stop polluting our environment?" In
the examples above, you should repeat the
first question but not the second one.

   Why repeat questions, even positive
ones? First, you will ensure that you heard
the question correctly. Second, you allow
the rest of the audience to hear the question and not hear only an answer given

seemingly out of context. Third, it allows you think time—mental time to begin preparing your answer.

4. ***Rephrase Negative Questions.***
You don't want to publicize a question that slams your company by repeating it over a loud speaker. Therefore, don't repeat explosive or negative questions—rather rephrase them to your advantage. In essence, rephrase the question the way you would like to have had it presented. For example, if you had been asked: "Why don't you guys stop polluting the environment?" You might rephrase it as follows: "The question had to do with the environment, and what we are doing about it." Such a lead-in allows you to now talk about the programs that your company sponsors to improve the environment, rather than get embroiled in an apology or argument.

5. ***Address the Entire Audience.***
Look at the person who asked you the question as you begin to answer it. However, after you repeat the question, engage the entire audience with sweeping eye contact. This keeps any one person from monopolizing the questions while at

the same time maintaining group involve-
ment in the Q-and-A.

6. **Be Brief.**
   Get to the point as quickly as you can. This
   will allow you to take more questions. Also,
   be aware that the audience has already had
   to sit through your speech and may be getting weary. Brief is better.

7. **If You Don't Know, Say So.**
   Within reason, audiences expect that you
   might not have answers to every question
   asked. But when you don't know an
   answer, simply admit it and indicate that
   you would be willing to find out the
   answer. However, if you promise to get
   back to them, make sure you ask the
   person to see you after the speech to get a
   phone number. Then be absolutely sure you
   call within the next day or two to answer
   the question. Word of the call will spread,
   and your credibility will soar long after the
   speech.

8. **Set a Limit on Questions.**
   You may want to agree on a wrap-up signal
   with the host or the master of ceremony
   ahead of time. However, either might get

caught up in the moment and may not be paying attention to you. Therefore, you will want to control the situation by saying, "I have time for one or two more questions.' This allows you to end on a positive note. For example, if you answer a question poorly or you get a no-win question, then take another one. If, on the other hand, you do an exceptional job, you may want to look at your watch and say, "I've taken enough of your time already—but I will remain after the speech to answer any other questions some of you might have." This allows you a graceful exit and tells those with hands still in the air that you'll not run away.

9. ***Make Your Responses Credible.***
Credibility comes from a number of techniques and here are a few: Whenever you can, quote outside and reliable experts and sources. If you do, your answers will have more sway: "The latest Roper Poll showed...." Drive home your themes. Keep coming back to the themes you want the audience to accept. Make numbers and stats easy to handle by rounding them off. Say about $1,000 instead of $998.82. Provide references to your experience and

expertise, "During my 15 years in the business, I've...."

10. *Learn to Bridge.*
When you're on a topic that you want to avoid, when you want to get back to your themes or when time is running out and you want to emphasize a particular point— use the bridging technique to change your direction. Bridging is merely shifting, by the speaker, to a new, preferred topic. For example, "That's an interesting observation, but I think the really crucial issue here is...."

TIP #3: PLAN FOR TOUGH SITUATIONS

1. *When No Questions Come.*
Most people hate to be the first to ask a question. As a consequence, often the first question never comes. This can lead to an embarrassing ending to a good speech. To avoid such a situation, arrange for someone in the audience ahead of time to ask a prepared question or have the host ask one or two. If that does not work, refer back to the most commonly asked questions: "One

of the most common questions I get from people is...." Finally, if still no questions come, provide a gracious wrap-up and sit down.

2. ***When Someone Gives a Speech Instead of Asking a Question.***
As the speaker, you're in charge. When some questioner uses a question as a soapbox from which to deliver a 10-minute speech, you will need to take control. The audience will not only signal you with their nonverbals (with their eyes and body movements), but will also expect you to keep this person from wasting their time. To set limits, politely interrupt and ask simply, "Excuse me, what exactly is your question?"

3. ***When You Get a Hostile Question.***
First, be as polite as you can; disagree with a smile: "Perhaps there has been a misunderstanding. Let me try to clarify...." Second, avoid arguments or embarrassing anyone—especially the hostile questioner. You have authority because you are the speaker, but if you use it to degrade, the audience may attack you and defend him or her. Third, if the situation escalates, first

turn to your host. Often a host will pop up and regain control. If this does not work, invite the person to continue the discussion with you after the speech: "Sir, in the interest of time, I'd like to invite you to discuss this matter with me after the speech...." Finally, be secure that precious few people ever heckle speakers, and when they do and won't quit, the audience usually attacks them when they get out of hand.

4. ***When You Are Asked Multiple Questions.***
"Will you do this? And then how will you handle that? Also, why did you do...?" Some people try to get every question they can out at once. Don't be confused. Either take each question one-by-one and ask that they be individually repeated, or better yet, answer only one of the questions—the one that you liked!

5. ***When You Are Asked a Hypothetical Question.***
Avoid it. Tell the audience you would rather deal with factual situations in which the variables are known than in the land of hypotheticals. For example, Question:

"What would you do if you were president?" Answer: "I'd rather respond to factual situations and what is—than what could, might or should be."

6. **When You Are Asked a Value-Loaded Question.**
When asked either what is the best or worst or if you're asked to rank anything—avoid it. If you answer directly, you will be assured of offending someone or a segment of the audience. It's a trap, so stay clear. Rather, say: "Among the most important priorities this year are...."

7. **When You Are Asked a Question with a Faulty Premise.**
Another trap you might find yourself falling into is to try a question that is based on a faulty premise. The old standby example is: "Do you still hit your wife?" Any answer you give is a loser. In these situations, immediately correct the faulty premise: "That's a baseless question, and I would like to correct it immediately before proceeding."

Answering questions at the conclusion of a speech is perhaps the most challenging part of the speech, yet the least practiced by public speakers. Unfortunately, poor performance at this stage of the speech can undermine all your speech preparation. When faced with a speech, remember the tips:

TIP #1: Anticipate questions.

TIP #2: Develop a strategy to handle questions.

TIP #3: Plan for tough situations.

Adhering to these tips will not make you totally bullet proof as a speaker, but they protect you from most rounds fired at you— and they will be fired.

THE TENTH RULE:

Publicize Your Speech

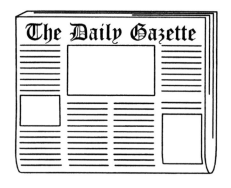

Considering the amount of time and energy you will invest in your speech, it makes sense to get the most mileage you can out of the presentation. While the neophyte might see the speech as a one-shot event, the experienced speaker merely sees the speech as one form of many communication opportunities. Indeed, a speech may serve multiple functions in the public affairs process.

This chapter will briefly explore how to prepare for speech publicity and how to execute it. The whole purpose is to show you how to get maximum exposure for every speech you deliver. In a way, your speech can be delivered over and over again, long after the microphone is turned off.

Other than the speech event itself, speech publicity opportunities have two places within the speech cycle: before and after the speech. Let's, therefore, explore each.

BEFORE THE SPEECH

What follows is a list of pre-speech publicity events that will build suspense and interest in your words well before you ever deliver them.

1. ***Send a Release to the Media.*** If you want
coverage, you must let the news media
know to whom, on what and when you are
speaking. Remember the requirements of
each form of news media: Newspapers
require print and photos where appropriate;
TV needs brief sound bites of catchy
phrases and later photo opportunities.
Radio, of course, needs simple 15 to 30
second sound bites, most of which can be
read over the phone.

2. ***Develop a Knockout Title.*** The more
expressive the title of your speech, the
more attention it will attract. Let's compare
two different titles:

Boring:	"Democracy and Communism—A Status Report"
Vibrant:	"Democracy's Silent Stranglehold on Communism"

Notice what a difference the title can make.
It will attract attention, and if there's
substance behind it—you will get the
coverage you want and deserve.

3. ***Mail Advance Copies to Trade Magazines.***
Most professions have a trade association
which has, as one of its primary duties, the
fostering of goodwill. Associations seek out
information from a number of sources in the
industry. From press releases to position
papers, associations scour the territory to
remain current and seize public relations
opportunities. To make their jobs easier,
send your speech to them. To help them
you may also want to provide a brief
summary—even a press release along with
the speech in which you highlight the main
points of the speech and perhaps several
memorable quotes. This does two things.
First, because most associations have
limited staff and space within their publica-
tions, you will save them time by synop-
sizing your speech and, therefore, you
stand a greater chance of getting publicity.
Second, you are more likely to be properly
quoted and more accurately represented if
you provide the basic document.

4. ***Keep Your Own Public Relations Staff
Informed.*** Make sure that your public
relations staff gets one of the first copies of
your speech. Through their regular news
contacts they can ensure that the media

becomes aware of your speech. By using contacts and the wire services, your staff can build public interest in your address long before you give it. Further, by having a copy of the draft, they will be better able to answer questions that might arise during the follow-up period.

AFTER THE SPEECH

Long after you have given your speech, it can have a life of its own. To ensure longevity and mileage from your words, try the following tips:

1. ***Arrange a Press Conference.*** Speeches provide a perfect time for press coverage because they often attract media attention. Why not use the opportunity to capture the moment and get extra mileage for the speech by entertaining questions from the media at a post-speech press conference. Remember, as a word of caution, that if you open up to the media, don't expect them to stick to issues pertaining to the speech unless you make that clear before you begin the press conference. Otherwise you will get questions on every controversial topic with which you or your company are associated.

If you plan to conduct a press conference after a speech, you should be sure that you have a public relations specialist with you to manage the conference and to keep you from getting in over your head. Your publicist can set the parameters for the conference and can both ward off and encourage questions as well as answer certain questions. *The Bottom Line:* Involve the PR office early—very early if you plan a press conference.

2. *Have Extra Copies Available.* If you've done a good job as a speaker, interest in your speech will be high directly following your address. Audiences are most motivated to do something after hearing a dynamic speech than at any other time. Therefore, seize the opportunity to hitchhike on their enthusiasm by providing copies of the speech for distribution, not only to the news media but also to the audience itself. If motivated, they will tend to promote and publish your remarks, either formally or informally. *Caution:* Don't hand out your remarks before a speech or you may lose part of your audience. They begin reading the speech instead of listening to you, and

eventually you may be distracted by their inattention to you.

3. ***Have Reprints of Your Speech Made.***
Having reprints made is an inexpensive way to give your speech life after delivery. By having such reprints available, you will be able to send them out in response to inquiries on the topic, and also they can be used for post-speech publicity. In fact, reprints should be sent to professional magazines like *Vital Speeches of the Day, Speechwriter's Newsletter* and any professional magazines or newsletters in your company's area of interest.

4. ***Use Excerpts for Company Magazines/ Newsletters.*** Don't miss the opportunity to reuse your speech again in the company newsletter or magazine. Often particular excerpts are especially germane to your internal audience and require little or no writing or thinking—only excerpting.

5. ***Save All Your Speeches for a Book.***
Consider each speech you give as a potential chapter to your book. What book? The one you never thought of. Consider how much time and energy goes into a single

speech and the many you may give on a variety of related topics over the years. They may well be the basis for a book on your topic of expertise. Don't fail to consider this option by keeping one final copy of every speech you deliver in a single folder. Periodically review them to see if you're working toward a theme—if so, arrange to give speeches on areas not yet explored. Thus, you will be "writing" a book as you speak—double duty is smart business.

EPILOGUE

Well, there's good news and bad news about this book. The good news is that it should help you know enough about speeches to be successful in your chosen profession. The bad news is that the book cannot do the work for you. Eventually, all the reading must stop and the doing start. You might start by properly screening, selecting and then giving speeches to acclimate yourself to the kind of rigor that comes from having a deadline. Thus, if you want to approach perfection you cannot just read these ten rules, you must live them.

INDEX

Steve Gladis, Ph.D.

The varied career of Dr. Steve Gladis includes academic, government, and military experience as well as civic service.

Dr. Gladis is a member of the University of Virginia's faculty and serves as the director of the University's Northern Virginia Center, which serves over 7,000 students with over 500 courses and programs. In his previous career, Dr. Gladis served as a Special Agent in the FBI. He taught at the FBI Academy, was the editor of the *FBI Law Enforcement Bulletin*, served as the chief of speechwriting for the director of the FBI and held a number of both headquarters and field-agent assignments around the country. He is also a former U.S. Marine Corps officer and a Vietnam Veteran.

Dr. Gladis has published numberous magazine and journal articles as well as eight books. A regular lecturer and speaker, Dr. Gladis consults with corporations and organizations in the area of training and development.

A committed civic and academic leader, Dr. Gladis serves on the Executive Board of the Fairfax County Chamber of Commerce, is the

chairman of the Board of Trustees of the
Washington Math Science Technology Public
Charter High School, and is a member of the
University of Virginia's Faculty Senate.